# THE POWER OF MINDFULNESS

BY ABBY COLICH

BLUE OWL
BOOKS

# TIPS FOR CAREGIVERS

Social and emotional learning (SEL) helps children manage emotions, create and achieve goals, maintain relationships, learn how to feel empathy, and make good decisions. The SEL approach will help children establish positive habits in communication, cooperation, and decision-making. By incorporating SEL in early reading, children will be better equipped to build confidence and foster positive peer networks.

## BEFORE READING

Talk to the reader about what mindfulness is and how to be mindful.

**Discuss:** What is one way you can practice mindfulness?

## AFTER READING

Talk to the reader about the physical and mental benefits of practicing mindfulness.

**Discuss:** How does mindfulness help your mind? How does it help your body?

## SEL GOAL

Children may have a difficult time understanding the benefits of mindfulness. Explain to them that regularly practicing mindfulness can cause certain reactions in the brain. Those reactions can help both their minds and bodies.

# TABLE OF CONTENTS

# CHAPTER 1

# WHAT IS MINDFULNESS?

Sit in a comfortable position. Close your eyes. Try to stay still. Relax your body and mind. Take deep breaths. How do you feel?

Paying attention to how you feel is one way to be **mindful**. When you are mindful, you focus on what is going on right now. You are aware of how your mind and body feel. Your thoughts are slowed. You are not doing too many things at once.

There are many ways to be mindful. You can practice mindfulness while walking by paying attention to the sights and smells around you. You can **meditate**. You can be mindful when you **interact** with others.

## MINDFUL RELATIONSHIPS

**Actively** listen when others speak. Pay attention to their **body language**. Think about how they might be feeling. Being mindful of others can help you learn **empathy**. It can build better relationships.

# CHAPTER 2

# BENEFITS OF MINDFULNESS

Mindfulness has many **benefits**. You may feel calmer. Your memory may get better. You might be able to focus more.

Scientists studied the brains of mindful people. They looked at the amygdala. This part of the brain helps us see **threats**. It is responsible for fear and **anxiety**. The amygdala is smaller in mindful people. It is less active. Mindful people experience less **stress**.

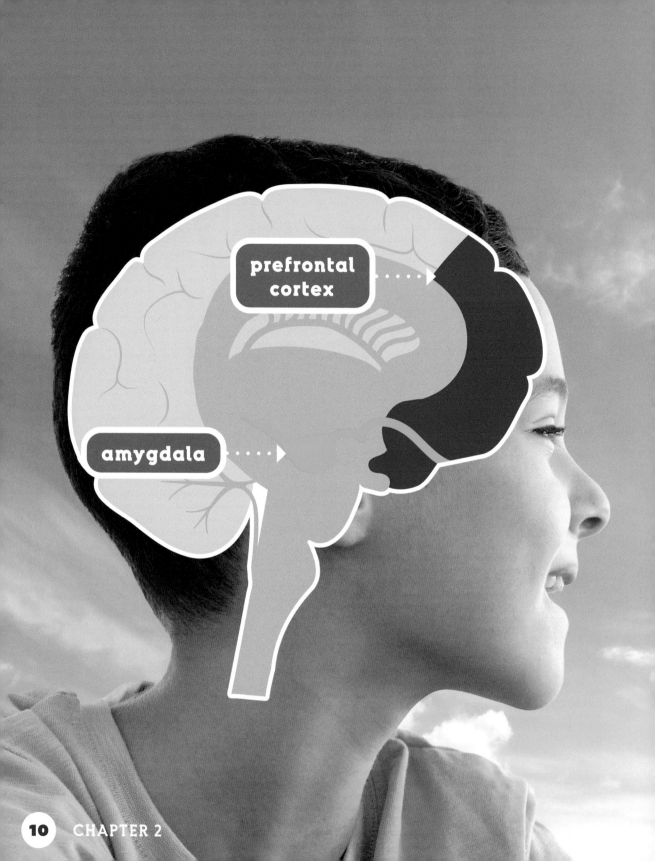

prefrontal cortex

amygdala

The amygdala connects to the prefrontal cortex. The prefrontal cortex helps control your **emotions**. Mindfulness activates and thickens your prefrontal cortex. It also strengthens the connection between the amygdala and prefrontal cortex. This can help you control your feelings.

Evan practices mindful walking every day. He has a spelling bee coming up. He feels calm and focused. He feels ready.

The hippocampus is another part of the brain. It helps with memory and learning. It thickens in mindful people. Scientists also study the anterior cingulate cortex. It is more active in people who meditate. It helps you **self-regulate**.

Meg practices mindful breathing. Today, she and her sister argued. Meg felt **frustrated**. She wanted to scream. Instead, she took a few deep breaths. She stayed calm. Later, Meg and her sister talked calmly about their argument.

hippocampus

anterior
cingulate
cortex

Scientists study how mindfulness helps the body. It can lower your **blood pressure**. This keeps your heart healthy. Practicing mindfulness can help you play your favorite sports and sleep better, too.

## MINDFULNESS AND HEALTH

Mindfulness is good for your **immune system**. Being mindful can keep you from getting sick. It can also help you heal faster and feel less pain.

# CHAPTER 3

# HOW TO BE MINDFUL

How can you be mindful? Try meditating in a comfortable, quiet place. Sit still. Repeat a word to yourself such as "calm" or "peace." Do this for a few minutes. How do you feel?

Mindful breathing is another way. Count to three as you breathe in. Then breathe out for three counts. This can help slow any racing thoughts.

It is hard to be mindful when your mind races. Try focusing on just one thing, like what you can hear. Or focus on one body part and how it feels. Focusing on just one thing can help slow your thoughts.

## BODY SCAN

A body scan is one way to practice mindfulness. Start at your feet. Notice how they feel. Move up to your legs and knees. Stop at each body part for a few moments until you reach the top of your head.

You can practice mindfulness anytime or anywhere. You can practice as you walk or sit at your desk. You can practice when with others. Even if you only practice a few minutes a day, you can still experience all the benefits!

# GOALS AND TOOLS

## GROW WITH GOALS

Practicing mindfulness has many benefits. Try these activities to help keep your mind and body healthy.

**Goal:** Be mindful every morning. Add a two-minute meditation or body scan to your morning routine.

**Goal:** Practice mindful walking. Focus on your surroundings while you walk instead of what is on your mind.

**Goal:** Create art mindfully. Notice how a paintbrush or pencil feels against the paper. Pay close attention to the colors. How do you feel as you create art?

## TRY THIS!

Engage your five senses. Whether you are sitting, standing, or walking, think about the things around you. What do you hear? What can you taste and smell? What do you see? What do the things around you feel like? Focusing on what you are experiencing through your five senses can help slow racing thoughts. It can help you be more aware of what is around you.

# GLOSSARY

**actively**
Engaged in action or activity.

**anxiety**
A feeling of worry or fear.

**benefits**
Things that produce good or helpful results or effects or that promote well-being.

**blood pressure**
The pressure put on arteries and veins by blood.

**body language**
Gestures or movements used to communicate with others.

**emotions**
Feelings, such as happiness, sadness, or anger.

**empathy**
The ability to understand and share the emotions and experiences of others.

**frustrated**
Annoyed or angry.

**immune system**
The body system that protects against disease and infection.

**interact**
To talk or do things with other people.

**meditate**
To think deeply and quietly.

**mindful**
A mentality achieved by focusing on the present moment and calmly recognizing and accepting your feelings, thoughts, and sensations.

**self-regulate**
To control yourself.

**stress**
Mental or emotional strain.

**threats**
Signs or possibilities that something harmful or dangerous may happen.

# TO LEARN MORE

**FACT SURFER**

## Finding more information is as easy as 1, 2, 3.

**1.** Go to www.factsurfer.com

**2.** Enter "**thepowerofmindfulness**" into the search box.

**3.** Choose your book to see a list of websites.

# INDEX

Blue Owl Books are published by Jump!, 5357 Penn Avenue South, Minneapolis, MN 55419, www.jumplibrary.com

Copyright © 2024 Jump! International copyright reserved in all countries. No part of this book may be reproduced in any form without written permission from the publisher.

Library of Congress Cataloging-in-Publication Data

Names: Colich, Abby, author.
Title: The power of mindfulness / by Abby Colich.
Description: Minneapolis, MN: Jump!, Inc., [2024]
Series: The power of positivity | Includes index.
Audience: Ages 7–10
Identifiers: LCCN 2023037415 (print)
LCCN 2023037416 (ebook)
ISBN 9798889966920 (hardcover)
ISBN 9798889966937 (paperback)
ISBN 9798889966944 (ebook)
Subjects: LCSH: Mindfulness (Psychology) –Juvenile literature. | Emotions in children–Juvenile literature. | Social learning–Juvenile literature.
Classification: LCC BF637.M56 C645 2024 (print)
LCC BF637.M56 (ebook)
DDC 158.1/3–dc23/eng/20230920
LC record available at https://lccn.loc.gov/2023037415
LC ebook record available at https://lccn.loc.gov/2023037416

Editor: Katie Chanez
Designer: Emma Almgren-Bersie
Content Consultant: Megan Kraemer, MSW, LICSW

Photo Credits: PeopleImages/iStock, cover; Khosrork/iStock, 1; Sakura Image Inc/Shutterstock, 3; fizkes/Shutterstock, 4; real444/iStock, 5; MesquitaFMS/iStock, 6–7; Pixel-Shot/Shutterstock, 8; katleho Seisa/iStock, 9; Larysa Dubinska/Shutterstock, 10–11; DarioGaona/iStock, 12–13; SolStock/iStock, 14–15; SewcreamStudio/iStock, 16; Anatoliy Karlyuk/Shutterstock, 17; mtreasure/iStock, 18–19; Pressmaster/Shutterstock, 20–21.

Printed in the United States of America at Corporate Graphics in North Mankato, Minnesota.